HOLIDAYS, FESTIVALS, & CELEBRATIONS

MARTIN LUTHER KING, JR. DAY

BY TRUDI STRAIN TRUEIT · ILLUSTRATED BY JOEL SNYDER

Published in the United States of America by The Child's World®
1980 Lookout Drive • Mankato, MN 56003-1705
800-599-READ • www.childsworld.com

ACKNOWLEDGMENTS

The Child's World®: Mary Berendes, Publishing Director

The Design Lab: Kathleen Petelinsek, Design and Page Production

Editorial Direction: Red Line Editorial, Patricia Stockland, Managing Editor

LIBRARY OF CONGRESS CATALOGING-IN-PUBLICATION DATA
   Trueit, Trudi Strain.
    Martin Luther King, Jr. Day / written by Trudi Strain Trueit ;
illustrated by Joel Snyder.
       p. cm. — (Holidays, festivals & celebrations)
   Includes bibliographical references and index.
   Audience: Grades K-3.
   ISBN-13: 978-1-59296-814-5 (library bound : alk. paper)
   ISBN-10: 1-59296-814-7 (library bound : alk. paper)
    1. Martin Luther King Day—Juvenile literature. 2. King, Martin
Luther 1929-1968—Juvenile literature. I. Snyder, Joel. II. Title.
III. Series.
   E185.97.K5T785 2007 2008
   394.261—dc22   2006103389

TABLE OF CONTENTS

CHAPTER ONE

AN AMERICAN HERO

Americans of many different races join hands. Together, they march down the street and sing. Come join the parade! It's Martin Luther King, Jr. Day.

Martin Luther King, Jr. was an important African-American leader. He worked to make sure all U.S. citizens were treated equally.

On the third Monday in January, Americans honor Martin Luther King, Jr. They remember a man whose courage helped change a nation.

Some cities hold parades on Martin Luther King, Jr. Day. Come march in the parade!

This country will not be a good place for any of us to live in unless we make it a good place for all of us to live in.

—Theodore Roosevelt (1858–1919), former U.S. president

CHAPTER TWO

BIRTH OF A LEADER

Martin Luther King, Jr. was born on January 15, 1929. His family called him M.L. for short. M.L. lived in Atlanta, Georgia, with his parents, grandparents, aunt, and older sister Christine. In 1930, M.L.'s brother Alfred was born.

Children of different races lived in M.L.'s neighborhood. They all played together. One day, M.L. and Alfred went to visit two white brothers as they had always done. But the boys said their parents wouldn't allow them to play with black children anymore.

M.L. ran to his mother. She said that some people didn't realize that beneath the skin everyone was the same. It was painful for M.L to lose his friends this way. He never forgot it.

Growing up in Atlanta, M.L played with children of other races.

M.L. was a good musician, athlete, and student. He started college at age 15.

CHAPTER THREE

DIFFERENT RACES, DIFFERENT RULES

When M.L. was growing up, black and white Americans were not treated equally. In some cities, it was against the law for blacks to go to the same places as whites. They could not attend the same schools or eat in the same restaurants. Elevators and drinking fountains had signs that read "Whites Only." This was called **segregation**.

Such treatment made M.L. angry at whites. M.L.'s father was a minister. He told his son that hatred wasn't the answer. Reverend King taught M.L. that he could love others and still stand up for what he believed.

M.L.'s father taught him to stand up peacefully for his beliefs.

You must be the change you wish to see in the world.
—Mahatma Ghandi
(1869–1948),
peace activist

Segregation laws were more common in southern states like Georgia, Alabama, Louisiana, and Mississippi. African Americans were once enslaved in these states.

CHAPTER FOUR

I HAVE A DREAM

After college, M.L. moved to Alabama and became a minister like his father. He married Coretta Scott. They had four children.

Dr. King, as he was now called, began speaking out against segregation. He led peaceful marches for **civil rights**, or equality. He gave **speeches**, too.

Dr. King led many marches for equal rights.

We hold these truths to be self-evident, that all men are created equal, that they are endowed by their Creator with certain unalienable Rights, that among these are Life, Liberty and the pursuit of Happiness.

—U.S. Declaration of Independence (1776)

Dr. King's most famous speech was called "I Have a Dream."

"I have a dream that one day this nation will rise up and live out the true meaning of its **creed**; we hold these truths to be self-evident that all men are created equal," he said. "I have a dream that my four little children will one day live in a nation where they will not be judged by the color of their skin but by the content of their **character**."

Dr. King quoted the U.S. Declaration of Independence in his famous speech.

CHAPTER FIVE

TAKING ACTION

D r. King's leadership made a difference. In 1964, U.S. President Lyndon Johnson signed the Civil Rights Act. It made segregation against the law.

Even so, some people didn't want things to change. On April 4, 1968, Dr. King was shot and killed. He was buried in Atlanta, Georgia, next to his grandmother.

In 1983, the U.S. Congress created a national holiday to honor Dr. Martin Luther King, Jr. They chose the third Monday in January so the date would fall on or near Dr. King's birthday.

President Johnson signed the Civil Rights Act in 1964.

I've seen the promised land. I may not get there with you. But I want you to know tonight, that we, as a people, will get to the promised land.
—Martin Luther King, Jr., "I've Been to the Mountaintop," April 3, 1968 (the day before his death)

CHAPTER SIX

CELEBRATING CIVIL RIGHTS

C hurch bells ring. Choirs sing angelic **hymns**. Across the nation, people gather on Martin Luther King, Jr. Day. They may watch a film of one of Dr. King's speeches. Older citizens often share what it was like to live during segregation.

Some Americans take part in peaceful marches. Others volunteer in their communities. They may pick up litter, paint over graffiti, or plant trees in a park.

Martin Luther King, Jr. Day is a time to remember the struggle for civil rights. It is a time to remember that every American citizen is equal and free.

America will never be destroyed from the outside. If we falter and lose our freedoms, it will be because we destroyed ourselves.
—Abraham Lincoln
(1809–1865)

Some people help in their communities on Martin Luther King, Jr. Day.

CHAPTER SEVEN

POETRY CORNER

When we allow freedom to ring, when we let it ring from every village and every hamlet, from every state and every city, we will be able to speed up that day when all of God's children, black men and white men, Jews and Gentiles, Protestants and Catholics, will be able to join hands and sing in the words of the old Negro spiritual, "Free at last, free at last. Thank God Almighty, we are free at last."

—Martin Luther King, Jr., "I Have a Dream," August 28, 1963

Courage is resistance to fear, mastery of fear—not absence of fear.
—Mark Twain (1835–1910), American author

We Wear the Mask

We wear the mask that grins and lies,
It hides our cheeks and shades our eyes, —
This debt we pay to human guile;
With torn and bleeding hearts we smile,
And mouth with myriad subtleties.
Why should the world be overwise,
In counting all our tears and sighs?
Nay, let them only see us, while
We wear the mask.
—Paul Lawrence Dunbar
*   (1872–1906), African-American poet*

We who believe in freedom cannot rest.
—Ella Baker, (1903–1986)

We've come to see the power of nonviolence. We've come to see that this method is not a weak method, for it's the strong man who can stand up amid opposition, who can stand up amid violence being inflicted upon him and not retaliate with violence.
—Martin Luther King, Jr., "Detroit Speech," June 23, 1963

CHAPTER EIGHT

SONGS OF UNITY

H ymns like these were often sung during U.S. civil rights marches in the 1950s and 1960s.

We Shall Overcome

We shall overcome
We shall overcome
We shall overcome some day

Chorus:
Oh, deep in my heart
I do believe
We shall overcome some day

We'll walk hand in hand
We'll walk hand in hand
We'll walk hand in hand some day

Chorus

We shall all be free
We shall all be free
We shall all be free some day

Chorus

This Little Light of Mine

This little light of mine,
I'm gonna let it shine.
This little light of mine,
I'm gonna let it shine.
This little light of mine,
I'm gonna let it shine,
Let it shine,
Let it shine,
Let it shine.

Joining in the Spirit of Martin Luther King, Jr. Day

• Talk to a grandparent or senior citizen about their experiences with segregation. Discuss how the civil rights movement changed attitudes toward African Americans and other groups.

• Listen to Dr. King's "I Have a Dream" speech. Write down your dreams. What are your hopes and goals for your country? How about for yourself? What can you do to be the change you wish to see in the world?

• Make the holiday a day of service. Get your friends together. Clean up trash or plant flowers in a neighborhood park.

• Visit a local historical museum with your family to learn more about Dr. Martin Luther King, Jr., his life, and the fight for American civil rights.

Making a Martin Luther King, Jr. Day Pin

Create your own pin to celebrate that American children of all races may live and play together.

What you need:

Scissors

6 inches of yarn in each of these colors: black, light brown, and yellow (for hair)

Toothpick

White craft glue

Three round wooden beads, about the size of a marble: one dark brown, one light brown, one white (each bead will be a head)

Six small wiggle eyes

Three tiny pom-poms (two black and one white)

Red permanent marker

One pin-back

Directions:

1. Cut each strip of yarn into six 1-inch pieces. (Black yarn for the dark brown bead, light brown yarn for the light brown bead, and yellow yarn for the white bead).
2. Use one end of the toothpick to dab glue inside the hole of each bead.
3. Use the other end of the toothpick to push the six ends of colored yarn into its bead.
4. Glue two wiggle eyes onto the "face" of each bead.
5. Glue a tiny pom-pom onto the bead for a nose.
6. Use the red marker to draw a mouth on each bed.
7. Glue the three beads together to make a triangle of faces.
8. Glue the pin-back to the back of the top bead.

Wear your pin proudly on Martin Luther King, Jr. Day!

Craft reprinted by permission of Kaboose, © Kaboose, Inc.

Words to Know

character—the quality of an individual's personality or reputation

civil rights—equality and freedom for all citizens of the United States of America

creed—a set of beliefs

hymns—songs of praise or honor

segregation—forcing different racial groups to live apart from one another

speeches—talks given to audiences

How to Learn More about
Martin Luther King, Jr. Day

At the Library

Farris, Christine King and Chris Soentpiet (illustrator). *My Brother Martin: A Sister Remembers Growing Up With the Reverend Dr. Martin Luther King, Jr.* New York: Simon & Schuster, 2003.

Meyers, Walter Dean, and Leonard Jenkins (illustrator). *I've Seen the Promised Land: The Life of Dr. Martin Luther King, Jr.* New York: HarperCollins, 2004.

Sexton, Colleen. *Let's Meet Martin Luther King, Jr.* Philadelphia, PA: Chelsea Clubhouse Books, 2004.

On the Web

Visit our Web site for lots of links about Martin Luther King, Jr. Day:

http://www.childsworld.com/links

NOTE TO PARENTS, TEACHERS, AND LIBRARIANS:
We routinely verify our Web links to make sure they're safe,
active sites—so encourage your readers to check them out!

ABOUT THE AUTHOR

Trudi Strain Trueit is a former television news reporter and weather forecaster. She has written more than forty fiction and non-fiction books for children. She lives in Everett, Washington.

ABOUT THE ILLUSTRATOR

Joel Snyder is a graduate of the Rhode Island School of Design. He has had a long career of illustrating magazines, books, and other projects for children and young adults. Joel lives in upstate New York, where he enjoys fishing and kayaking in the Adirondack Mountains when he's not at his drawing board.

Index